The MISEDUCATION of the Negro in the 21st Century

Middle School Teacher's Edition by Cedric A. Washington

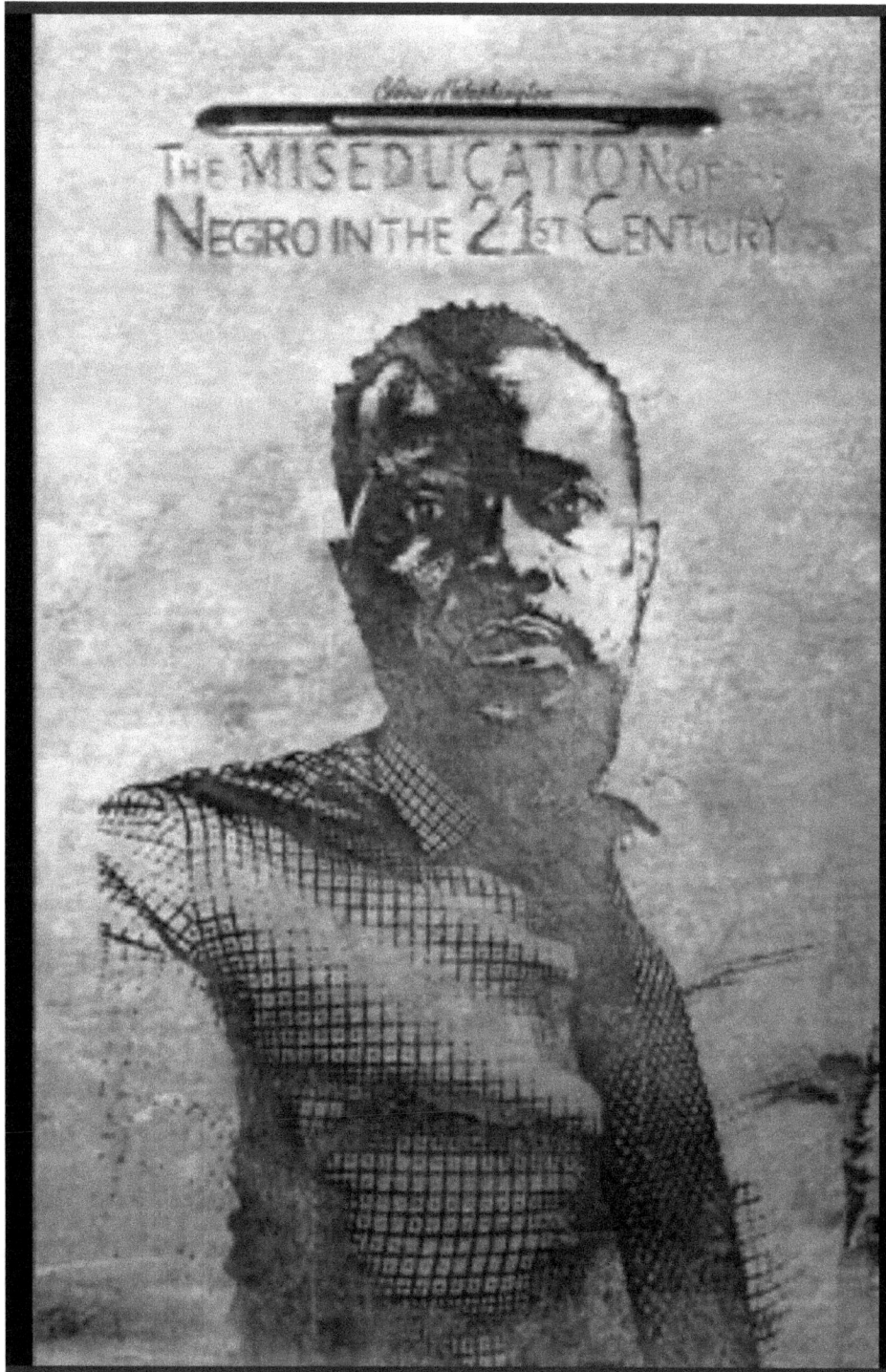

The MISEDUCATION of the Negro in the 21st Century – High School Student Workbook

Who Lives Like This?! Publishing LLC
www.nerdyouthservices.org

ISBN: 978-1-970680-00-3 (Hardcover)

Cover design and interior layout by
Who Lives Like This?! Publishing LLC Design Team

Printed in the United States of America

First Edition — 2025

Dedication

This work is dedicated to every young mind determined to break free from the chains of miseducation. To the students who question, the teachers who empower, and the ancestors whose sacrifices paved the road we walk today.

May this guide serve as a light, a weapon, and a foundation.
Never forget — you were born to lead, not follow.
The world is your classroom. The truth is your legacy.

- Cedric A. Washington
Author. Educator. Revolutionary.

Middle School TEACHER'S EDITION

Preface Unit — *The Miseducation of the Negro in the 21st Century*

Teach Like Ced Series
Knowledge of SELF (Social Empowerment Learning Framework)
Grade Band: 6–8

UNIT OVERVIEW (Teacher Only)

Central Idea (from the text)

Education systems prioritize **models, standards, and compliance** over **cultural competency, truth, and lived experience**, resulting in the continued **miseducation** of Black students and communities.

Author's Purpose

Cedric A. Washington challenges educators to question **who controls education, what is being taught**, and **why culture and knowledge of self have been excluded**, calling for courage, liberation, and ownership of education.

STANDARDS ALIGNMENT (District-Ready)

ELA (Grades 6–8)

- Cite textual evidence to support analysis of informational text
- Determine central ideas and explain how they are developed
- Analyze word choice and figurative language
- Write arguments supported by evidence from the text
- Engage effectively in collaborative discussions

Social Studies

- Analyze systems and institutions
- Examine power, authority, and governance
- Evaluate historical and cultural perspectives
- Understand cause-and-effect relationships in society

SEL — Knowledge of SELF Alignment

SELF Mastery Focus:

- **SELF Conscience** (identity, awareness, purpose)
- **Social Conscience** (community, systems, responsibility)

TEXT SEGMENTATION (NO EDITS)

Preface Excerpt A

- "The academic system known as education can stifle the pedagogy of the best teachers…"
- "…urban education is equivalent to Soul Food."

Preface Excerpt B

- "I was institutionalized in the constraints of traditional education…"
- "…schools pride themselves on a model versus listening to the expert, me."

Preface Excerpt C

- "We graduate kids that are not academically prepared…"
- "…it is time to get courageous and become free."

VOCABULARY (FROM THE TEXT ONLY)

Teachers: Do not pre-teach definitions. Students derive meaning from context.

Word/Phrase	Context-Based Meaning (Student-Derived)
pedagogy	How teaching is done within a system
ramifications	Consequences of teaching under state standards
mainstream	Dominant or widely accepted systems
curriculum	What is formally taught in schools
cultural competency	Ability to understand and teach students' culture
urban education	Schooling in under-resourced communities
Soul Food	Metaphor for making something meaningful from scraps
institutionalized	Conditioned by a system
compliant	Following rules without questioning

Word/Phrase	Context-Based Meaning (Student-Derived)
data driven	Focused on documentation and numbers
redirect	Correcting behavior and moving forward
insubordinate	Seen as disobedient to authority
model	A system schools value over people
perpetuate	Continue harmful practices
miseducation	Harmful or incorrect education
slavery	Control against one's internal knowledge
liberation	Becoming free from control
knowledge	Information and experience that creates intelligence

CLOSE READING QUESTIONS

(All answers must cite the text)

Literal Understanding

1. According to Washington, how do **state standards** impact teachers' pedagogy?
2. What does the author mean when he says, **"urban education is equivalent to Soul Food"**?

Author's Craft & Language

3. Why does Washington use metaphors like **"water into wine"** and **"water into Hennessey"**?
4. How does repetition of **"I am a free man"** shape the tone of the Preface?

Structural & Argument Analysis

5. How does Washington contrast **models** with **listening to experts**?
6. Why does the author describe documentation and discipline systems as harmful?

IDEAL RESPONSES (TEXT-DEPENDENT)

Responses quote or directly reference Washington's language.

- Washington explains that pedagogy is **stifled** because teachers must teach within the **ramifications of state standards**, even when those standards lack cultural competency.
- The **Soul Food** metaphor shows how Black educators are expected to create excellence despite **scraps, lack of resources, and undervalued feelings**.

- "Water into Hennessey" represents producing something **harmful** instead of transformative when forced into fake systems.
- The phrase **"I am a free man"** signals liberation from institutional control and intellectual slavery.

WRITING TASKS

Text-Based Constructed Response

Prompt:
How does Cedric A. Washington define the difference between **education** and **knowledge** in the Preface? Use evidence from the text.

Extended Writing (Argument)

Prompt:
Using Washington's Preface, argue whether compliance-based education can truly serve Black students. Support your claim using at least two direct references to the text.

DISCUSSION PROTOCOL (Socratic)

Anchor Question:

"Can you be educated and still be clueless?"

Students must:

- Reference Washington's definition of **slavery**
- Respond directly to peers
- Cite exact language from the Preface

ASSESSMENT RUBRIC (Preface)

Category	Points
Textual Evidence	10
Understanding of Author's Claim	10
Vocabulary in Context	5

Category	Points
Critical Reasoning	5
Total	**30**

TEACHER FACILITATION NOTES

- Do **not** sanitize language.
- Allow students to wrestle with discomfort.
- Emphasize **reading the author, not reacting to assumptions**.
- Reinforce that this is **informational text**, not opinion writing.

KNOWLEDGE OF SELF CONNECTION (Teacher-Facing)

SELF Conscience:
Students examine identity, freedom, and internal truth.

Social Conscience:
Students analyze systems, control, and responsibility.

Middle School TEACHER'S EDITION

Chapter 1 — Privilege

The Miseducation of the Negro in the 21st Century
Teach Like Ced Series
Knowledge of SELF (Social Empowerment Learning Framework)
Grade Band: 6–8

UNIT OVERVIEW (Teacher Only)

Central Idea (from the text)

Privilege in America is rooted in **historical design, constitutional access, and systemic structures** that automatically benefit white people while denying Black people equal preparation, resources, and cultural affirmation—especially in education.

Author's Purpose

Cedric A. Washington exposes how **charter schools, mainstream standards, and white liberal authority** perpetuate miseducation by ignoring history, culture, and knowledge of self, while calling for accountability, advocacy, and cultural leadership from those inside the system.

STANDARDS ALIGNMENT (District-Ready)

ELA (Grades 6–8)

- Cite textual evidence to support analysis of informational text
- Determine central ideas and explain how they are developed
- Analyze how word choice and quotations shape meaning and tone
- Write arguments supported with evidence from the text
- Participate in collaborative discussions using evidence

Social Studies

- Analyze historical systems and institutions
- Examine power, authority, and governance
- Understand cause-and-effect relationships
- Evaluate cultural and historical perspectives

Knowledge of SELF Alignment

SELF Mastery Focus:

- **SELF Conscience** (identity, awareness, history)
- **Social Conscience** (systems, privilege, accountability)

TEXT SEGMENTATION (NO EDITS)

Excerpt A — Educational Structures

- "There has been a deficit of learning in black America…"
- "…pop up shop institutions known as charter schools…"

Excerpt B — Historical Foundation

- "When the constitution was written in 1776…"
- "…psychologically enslaved."

Excerpt C — Culture and Control

- "This blueprint established propaganda…"
- "…lack of knowledge of self."

Excerpt D — Call to Action

- "To the white liberal teacher…"
- "…we must be led by us. We must be taught by us."

VOCABULARY

(Words and phrases appear directly in Chapter 1)

Students determine meaning from context.

Word / Phrase	Context-Based Meaning
deficit of learning	Ongoing lack of proper education
pop up shop institutions	Charter schools rapidly placed in communities
charter schools	Alternative schools dominating urban education
public school systems	Traditional schools being diminished

Word / Phrase	Context-Based Meaning
academic disproportionality	Unequal educational outcomes
mainstream education	Dominant educational system
qualifications	Credentials to teach
miseducation	Education that harms or misleads
privilege	Automatic access and advantage
constitutional layout	Foundation of American law
psychologically enslaved	Mentally controlled after slavery
propaganda	Messages shaping false beliefs
superiority	Elevated status
inferiority	Lowered status
systematic structure	Designed systems of control
glass ceiling	Invisible limit to success
knowledge of self	Understanding identity and origin
advocate	Speak and act in support
supplement	Provide what is missing
African American Studies	Required historical education
independence	Self-determination

CLOSE READING QUESTIONS

(All responses must cite Chapter 1 directly)

Literal Understanding

1. According to Washington, what changes occurred in urban education starting in the 1990s?
2. How does the author describe the role of charter schools in Black communities?

Author's Craft & Language

3. Why does Washington title this chapter **"Privilege"**?
4. How does the author use historical dates (1776, 1865) to support his argument?

Structural & Argument Analysis

5. How does Washington connect **education**, **history**, and **psychological enslavement**?
6. Why does the author argue that African American Studies should be required?

IDEAL RESPONSES (TEXT-DEPENDENT)

- Washington explains that charter schools **dominated urban education** while public school systems diminished, creating academic disproportionality.
- The chapter is titled **Privilege** because white people are "automatically privy" to America's constitutional promise.
- Historical references show that freedom was delayed and incomplete, leading to **psychological enslavement**.
- The author argues African American Studies is necessary because slavery and miseducation are foundational to American history.

WRITING TASKS

Constructed Response

Prompt:
How does Cedric A. Washington explain the relationship between privilege and education in Chapter 1? Use evidence from the text.

Extended Argument

Prompt:
Using Chapter 1, argue whether mainstream education adequately serves Black students. Support your claim with direct textual evidence.

DISCUSSION PROTOCOL

Anchor Question:

"Why does Washington argue that being white in America is a form of privilege?"

Rules:

- Cite the text
- Respond directly to peers
- No personal attacks; focus on evidence

ASSESSMENT RUBRIC — Chapter 1

Category	Points
Textual Evidence	10
Understanding of Privilege	10
Vocabulary in Context	5
Critical Reasoning	5
Total	**30**

TEACHER FACILITATION NOTES

- Maintain academic tone while honoring cultural truth.
- Do not soften historical language.
- Emphasize **systems**, not individual blame.
- Reinforce that this is **informational analysis**, not opinion.

KNOWLEDGE OF SELF CONNECTION

- **SELF Conscience:** Understanding identity and history
- **Social Conscience:** Recognizing systemic privilege and responsibility

Middle School TEACHER'S EDITION

Chapter 2 — Figurehead

The Miseducation of the Negro in the 21st Century
Teach Like Ced Series
Knowledge of SELF (Social Empowerment Learning Framework)
Grade Band: 6–8

UNIT OVERVIEW (Teacher Only)

Central Idea (from the text)

Figurehead leadership in Black education places Black principals in visible positions of authority **without real power**, forcing them to enforce policies that continue the miseducation and exploitation of Black students in order to maintain job security and institutional approval.

Author's Purpose

Cedric A. Washington exposes how **Black leadership within miseducated systems** often functions as symbolic compliance rather than transformative authority, and challenges Black principals to awaken their conscience and lead culturally, not administratively.

STANDARDS ALIGNMENT (District-Ready)

ELA (Grades 6–8)

- Cite textual evidence to analyze informational text
- Determine central ideas and how they develop
- Analyze quotations and rhetorical impact
- Write arguments using text-based evidence
- Engage in structured academic discussion

Social Studies

- Analyze leadership, authority, and power
- Examine institutional systems and governance
- Evaluate cause-and-effect relationships
- Understand historical continuity and change

Knowledge of SELF Alignment

SELF Mastery Focus:

- **SELF Governing** (leadership, decision-making, accountability)
- **Social Conscience** (systems, power, responsibility)

TEXT SEGMENTATION (NO EDITS)

Excerpt A — Figurehead Defined

- "I don't always agree with the rules…"
- "…a nominal leader or head without real power."

Excerpt B — Historical Context

- Woodson quote (1933)
- "the Negro's mind has been all but perfectly enslaved…"

Excerpt C — Black Principals

- "Black principals in education are the epitome…"
- "…just the face of the business."

Excerpt D — Discipline & Control

- "Sweat the small stuff…"
- "…school to prison pipeline…"

Excerpt E — Call to Conscience

- "To the black principal…"
- "…knowledge of self."

VOCABULARY

(All words and phrases appear directly in Chapter 2)

Students determine meaning from context.

Word / Phrase	Context-Based Meaning
figurehead	Leader in name only
nominal leader	Title without authority
authority	Power to make decisions
enslaved mind	Trained to think for the system
mis-educated	Harmfully trained
badge of honor	Status gained through compliance
job security	Protection of position
implement	Carry out orders
dysfunctionality	Fear of being seen as ineffective
exploit	Use harmfully
sweat the small stuff	Extreme discipline focus
school to prison pipeline	Policies pushing students to incarceration
zero-tolerance	No flexibility in discipline
tyrannical	Oppressive
doctrine	Rules to be followed
house negro	Symbolic servant role
conscience	Moral awareness
village	Collective responsibility
hamster wheel	Repetitive, unproductive cycle
glass ceiling	Invisible limit to success

CLOSE READING QUESTIONS

(All answers must cite Chapter 2 directly)

Literal Understanding

1. How does the author define a **figurehead**?
2. According to Washington, what position do Black principals often occupy within schools?

Author's Craft & Language

3. Why does Washington include the Woodson quote from 1933?
4. How does the phrase **"badge of honor"** function ironically in the chapter?

Structural & Argument Analysis

5. How does fear of dysfunctionality influence leadership behavior?

6. Why does Washington compare figurehead principals to the **house negro**?

IDEAL RESPONSES (TEXT-DEPENDENT)

- A figurehead is described as a **nominal leader without real power**.
- Black principals are placed **between a rock and a hard place**, forced to implement harmful policies.
- The Woodson quote demonstrates that miseducation is **not new** and continues into the 21st Century.
- The **house negro** comparison highlights symbolic leadership used to enforce oppression.
- Zero-tolerance discipline contributes to the **school to prison pipeline**.

WRITING TASKS

Constructed Response

Prompt:
How does Cedric A. Washington explain the danger of figurehead leadership in Black education? Use evidence from Chapter 2.

Extended Argument

Prompt:
Using Chapter 2, argue whether Black principals have real power within miseducated systems. Support your claim with textual evidence.

DISCUSSION PROTOCOL

Anchor Question:

"Can leadership exist without power?"

Rules:

- Cite the text
- Address ideas, not individuals
- Use Washington's terminology

ASSESSMENT RUBRIC — Chapter 2

Category	Points
Textual Evidence	10
Understanding of Leadership	10
Vocabulary in Context	5
Critical Reasoning	5
Total	**30**

TEACHER FACILITATION NOTES

- Emphasize **systems over personalities**
- Maintain historical and cultural accuracy
- Allow discomfort; it signals engagement
- Reinforce leadership as **responsibility**, not title

KNOWLEDGE OF SELF CONNECTION

- **SELF Governing:** Leadership with conscience
- **Social Conscience:** Accountability to the community

Middle School TEACHER'S EDITION

Chapter 3 — Knowledge vs. Education

The Miseducation of the Negro in the 21st Century
Teach Like Ced Series
Knowledge of SELF (Social Empowerment Learning Framework)
Grade Band: 6–8

UNIT OVERVIEW (Teacher Only)

Central Idea (from the text)

Education is **systematic instruction** controlled by institutions, while knowledge is **information, experience, and understanding** that develops intelligence, wisdom, and the ability to think critically. When education is controlled by an oppressor and separated from identity and culture, it produces miseducation.

Author's Purpose

Cedric A. Washington distinguishes between **being educated** and **having knowledge**, exposing how mainstream education—especially through generic social-emotional learning models—fails the so-called African American student by ignoring identity, culture, and knowledge of self.

STANDARDS ALIGNMENT (District-Ready)

ELA (Grades 6–8)

- Cite textual evidence to support analysis of informational text
- Determine and analyze central ideas
- Analyze how definitions and explanations develop an argument
- Write arguments supported by evidence
- Engage in collaborative academic discussions

Social Studies

- Examine systems of control and power
- Analyze social structures and institutions
- Understand cultural identity and social conditioning

- Evaluate cause-and-effect relationships

Knowledge of SELF Alignment

SELF Mastery Focus:

- **SELF Conscience** (identity, self-awareness)
- **SELF Governing** (critical thinking, decision-making)
- **Social Conscience** (empowerment, responsibility)

TEXT SEGMENTATION (NO EDITS)

Excerpt A — Definitions

- "Knowledge is defined as facts, information, and skills…"
- "Education is defined as the process of receiving or giving systematic instruction…"

Excerpt B — Control and Miseducation

- "If your oppressor controls your academic intelligence…"
- "…that can result in a miseducation."

Excerpt C — SEL Critique

- "The Collaborative Academic Social Emotional Learning model known as CASEL…"
- "…one size fits all approach…"

Excerpt D — Identity and Culture

- "How can one truly have self-awareness if you do not have proper identity?"
- "…preconceived notion."

Excerpt E — Knowledge of SELF Framework

- "Knowledge of SELF (Social Empowerment Learning Framework)…"
- "Love Yourself (The Skin You're In)…"

VOCABULARY

(Words and phrases appear directly in Chapter 3)

Students determine meaning using context from the text.

Word / Phrase	Context-Based Meaning
knowledge	Facts, information, and skills gained through experience
education	Systematic instruction through schools
intelligence	Ability to acquire and apply knowledge
miseducation	Harmful or incorrect education
oppressor	One who controls learning and information
systematic	Organized and controlled
CASEL	Social Emotional Learning model
SEL	Social Emotional Learning
self-awareness	Understanding oneself internally
identity	Distinguishing character of a person
culture	Shared characteristics shaping behavior
over generalizing	Treating groups as the same
preconceived notion	Assumptions based on identity
cognitive dissonance	Conflict between beliefs and information
melanin	Skin pigmentation
complexion	Skin tone
empowerment	Gaining strength and control
wisdom	Ability to use knowledge intelligently
Knowledge of SELF	Curriculum focused on identity and empowerment
Self-Conscience	First mastery step of SELF
Social Empowerment	Building self and community strength

CLOSE READING QUESTIONS

(All responses must cite Chapter 3 directly)

Literal Understanding

1. How does Washington define **knowledge** and **education**?
2. According to the text, who controls academic intelligence in mainstream education?

Author's Craft & Language

3. Why does Washington include dictionary definitions at the beginning of the chapter?
4. How does the phrase **"one size fits all"** critique SEL models?

Structural & Argument Analysis

5. Why does Washington argue that identity is missing from self-awareness?
6. How does the **Love Yourself (The Skin You're In)** lesson demonstrate true knowledge?

IDEAL RESPONSES (TEXT-DEPENDENT)

- Washington defines **education** as systematic instruction and **knowledge** as information and experience that creates intelligence.
- He argues miseducation occurs when an **oppressor controls academic intelligence**.
- Dictionary definitions clarify distinctions and prevent misunderstanding.
- The **one size fits all** approach ignores culture and identity.
- Identity is necessary for self-awareness because culture shapes intelligence.
- The skin tone lesson empowers students by teaching them to identify accurately and intentionally.

WRITING TASKS

Constructed Response

Prompt:
How does Cedric A. Washington explain the difference between knowledge and education in Chapter 3? Use evidence from the text.

Extended Argument

Prompt:
Using Chapter 3, argue whether mainstream education can create true self-awareness. Support your argument with textual evidence.

DISCUSSION PROTOCOL

Anchor Question:

"Can someone be educated and still be miseducated?"

Guidelines:

- Use Washington's definitions
- Cite exact language
- Respond directly to peers' claims

ASSESSMENT RUBRIC — Chapter 3

Category	Points
Textual Evidence	10
Understanding of Knowledge vs. Education	10
Vocabulary in Context	5
Critical Reasoning	5
Total	**30**

TEACHER FACILITATION NOTES

- Emphasize definitions before interpretation
- Do not substitute alternative SEL language
- Reinforce culture as central to intelligence
- Maintain informational text lens

KNOWLEDGE OF SELF CONNECTION

- **SELF Conscience:** Identity and awareness
- **SELF Governing:** Thinking independently
- **Social Conscience:** Empowering others

Middle School TEACHER'S EDITION

Chapter 4 — Culture = Intelligence = Behavior

The Miseducation of the Negro in the 21st Century
Teach Like Ced Series
Knowledge of SELF (Social Empowerment Learning Framework)
Grade Band: 6–8

UNIT OVERVIEW (Teacher Only)

Central Idea (from the text)

Culture creates intelligence, and intelligence produces behavior. When culture is intentionally stripped, distorted, or replaced, the resulting intelligence and behavior reflect trauma, fear, survival, and miseducation across generations.

Author's Purpose

Cedric A. Washington explains how **historical psychological conditioning**, cultural removal, and environmental control shaped the intelligence and behavior of the so-called African American people, and how those effects continue to manifest in modern communities, education, and identity.

STANDARDS ALIGNMENT (District-Ready)

ELA (Grades 6–8)

- Cite textual evidence to support analysis of informational text
- Determine central ideas and trace how they are developed
- Analyze how quotations and historical references shape meaning
- Write explanatory and argumentative responses using evidence
- Engage in collaborative discussions grounded in text

Social Studies

- Analyze historical systems of control
- Examine culture, identity, and social conditioning
- Understand cause-and-effect relationships across time
- Evaluate how environment influences behavior

Knowledge of SELF Alignment

SELF Mastery Focus:

- **SELF Conscience** (identity, origin, awareness)
- **Social Conscience** (community, environment, responsibility)

TEXT SEGMENTATION (NO EDITS)

Excerpt A — Psychological Conditioning

- Willie Lynch quotation
- "shave off the brute's mental history…"

Excerpt B — Culture Defined

- "Culture being the attitudes and behavior characteristic…"
- "This culture developed an intelligence…"

Excerpt C — Rearing and Survival

- "Rearing was cultural…"
- "…raise her children accordingly."

Excerpt D — Modern Manifestations

- "In the modern day, we see the manifestations…"
- "…passed on from generation to generation…"

Excerpt E — Environment and Outcome

- "The culture in the 'hoods'…"
- "…product of your environment."

VOCABULARY

(All words and phrases appear directly in Chapter 4)

Students determine meaning using context from the text.

Word / Phrase	Context-Based Meaning
culture	Attitudes and behavior of a group
intelligence	Ability to acquire and apply knowledge
behavior	Actions shaped by intelligence
rearing	How children are raised
Willie Lynch	Slave owner tied to psychological control
mental history	Original cultural knowledge
illusion	False reality created to distract
orbit	Separate agendas or issues
slave culture	System of fear and control
submissive	Obedient through fear
survival	Acting to stay alive
division	Separation within a group
depreciation	Loss of value
paranoia	Fear passed through generations
insecurity	Doubt about self-worth
complexion	Skin tone
environment	Surroundings shaping behavior
normalcy	What is considered usual
product of your environment	Result of conditions around you
miseducation	Harmful conditioning
fixed state	Condition difficult to escape
knowledge of self	Understanding identity and origin

CLOSE READING QUESTIONS

(All responses must cite Chapter 4 directly)

Literal Understanding

1. How does the author define **culture** in this chapter?
2. What role did fear play in shaping slave behavior?

Author's Craft & Language

3. Why does Washington include the Willie Lynch quotation?
4. How does the phrase **"floating balls in a vacuum"** help explain division?

Structural & Argument Analysis

5. How does rearing influence intelligence and behavior?
6. How does Washington connect historical trauma to modern insecurity?

IDEAL RESPONSES (TEXT-DEPENDENT)

- Culture is defined as **the attitudes and behavior characteristic of a particular social group**.
- Fear was used to enforce submissive behavior and survival intelligence.
- The Willie Lynch quotation explains deliberate psychological conditioning.
- "Floating balls in a vacuum" represents disconnected agendas that divide people.
- Rearing determines how intelligence develops and how behavior is expressed.
- Insecurities about complexion and identity are linked to past cultural removal.

WRITING TASKS

Constructed Response

Prompt:
Explain how Cedric A. Washington connects culture, intelligence, and behavior in Chapter 4. Use evidence from the text.

Extended Argument

Prompt:
Using Chapter 4, argue whether behavior can change without changing culture. Support your argument with textual evidence.

DISCUSSION PROTOCOL

Anchor Question:

"Are people born with intelligence, or is it created by culture?"

Guidelines:

- Use only the text
- Reference specific examples
- Respond respectfully and analytically

ASSESSMENT RUBRIC — Chapter 4

Category	Points
Textual Evidence	10
Understanding of Culture	10
Vocabulary in Context	5
Critical Reasoning	5
Total	**30**

TEACHER FACILITATION NOTES

- Emphasize cause-and-effect across generations
- Avoid simplifying historical trauma
- Reinforce environment as instructional
- Maintain academic tone and rigor

KNOWLEDGE OF SELF CONNECTION

- **SELF Conscience:** Identity and awareness
- **Social Conscience:** Responsibility to environment and community

Middle School TEACHER'S EDITION

Chapter 5 — Parents and the Environment

The Miseducation of the Negro in the 21st Century
Teach Like Ced Series
Knowledge of SELF (Social Empowerment Learning Framework)
Grade Band: 6–8

UNIT OVERVIEW (Teacher Only)

Central Idea (from the text)

Parents and the environment shape intelligence, behavior, and outcomes across generations. When parents are misinformed and environments are unstable, children inherit patterns of behavior that contribute to the continuation of miseducation and community dysfunction.

Author's Purpose

Cedric A. Washington explains how **historical trauma, psychological conditioning, absence of Black male leadership, and community breakdown** influence parenting, student behavior, and educational outcomes in the 21st Century, calling for accountability and collective ownership.

STANDARDS ALIGNMENT (District-Ready)

ELA (Grades 6–8)

- Cite textual evidence to analyze informational text
- Determine central ideas and explain how they are developed
- Analyze how historical references support arguments
- Write arguments supported by evidence
- Participate in structured academic discussions

Social Studies

- Examine family and community structures
- Analyze cause-and-effect relationships
- Understand historical trauma and social conditioning
- Evaluate environmental influences on behavior

Knowledge of SELF Alignment

SELF Mastery Focus:

- **SELF Conscience** (identity, awareness)
- **Social Conscience** (community responsibility)
- **Good People Skills** (respect, accountability)

TEXT SEGMENTATION (NO EDITS)

Excerpt A — Knowing Better

- "When you know better, you do better."
- "But what if you really do not know better?"

Excerpt B — Psychological Conditioning

- Willie Lynch references
- "Keep the body and destroy the mind."

Excerpt C — Black Male Absence

- "The male, the man, is the leader…"
- "…higher rates of absenteeism in the homes…"

Excerpt D — Parenting and Behavior

- "That's how they are at home."
- "…behavior of black students…"

Excerpt E — Community Accountability

- "The black community parented each other's children…"
- "…the accountability of our environment."

VOCABULARY

(Words and phrases appear directly in Chapter 5)

Students determine meaning from context.

Word / Phrase	Context-Based Meaning
environment	Surroundings shaping behavior
intelligence	Ability to acquire and apply knowledge
behavior	Actions learned and repeated
psychological effect	Mental impact of experiences
dominant	Position of leadership
absenteeism	Absence from the home
role models	Examples to follow
accountability	Responsibility for actions
disrespect	Lack of regard for authority
vulgarity	Offensive language
discipline	Behavioral expectations
school to prison pipeline	System pushing students toward incarceration
intervention	Action to change behavior
community	Collective group of people
normalcy	What is considered usual
environment/ culture	Shared behaviors and values
misinformed	Lacking accurate knowledge
miseducation	Harmful or incorrect education
accountability of environment	Responsibility for community outcomes

CLOSE READING QUESTIONS

(All responses must cite Chapter 5 directly)

Literal Understanding

1. How does Washington explain the phrase "When you know better, you do better"?
2. According to the text, what role does the Black man traditionally play in the family?

Author's Craft & Language

3. Why does Washington revisit the Willie Lynch theory in this chapter?
4. How does the phrase "That's how they are at home" function in the argument?

Structural & Argument Analysis

5. How does absenteeism affect children's behavior and education?
6. Why does Washington argue that communities must reclaim accountability?

IDEAL RESPONSES (TEXT-DEPENDENT)

- Washington questions whether people can "do better" if they were never taught better.
- He identifies the Black man as leader, protector, and provider of the family.
- The Willie Lynch reference explains generational psychological conditioning.
- "That's how they are at home" shows how behavior is normalized.
- Absenteeism leads to lack of role models and negative behavior patterns.
- Community accountability once corrected behavior and supported youth.

WRITING TASKS

Constructed Response

Prompt:
Explain how parents and the environment influence intelligence and behavior in Chapter 5. Use evidence from the text.

Extended Argument

Prompt:
Using Chapter 5, argue whether schools alone can correct behavior shaped by home and environment. Support your argument with textual evidence.

DISCUSSION PROTOCOL

Anchor Question:

"Can schools fix problems created at home and in the community?"

Guidelines:

- Cite the text
- Focus on systems, not individuals

- Use Washington's language

ASSESSMENT RUBRIC — Chapter 5

Category	Points
Textual Evidence	10
Understanding of Environment	10
Vocabulary in Context	5
Critical Reasoning	5
Total	**30**

TEACHER FACILITATION NOTES

- Maintain sensitivity while addressing hard truths
- Emphasize shared responsibility
- Avoid blaming students
- Reinforce cultural context

KNOWLEDGE OF SELF CONNECTION

- **SELF Conscience:** Awareness of self and upbringing
- **Social Conscience:** Responsibility to community
- **Good People Skills:** Respect and accountability

Middle School TEACHER'S EDITION

Chapter 6 — Hip-Hop

The Miseducation of the Negro in the 21st Century
Teach Like Ced Series
Knowledge of SELF (Social Empowerment Learning Framework)
Grade Band: 6–8

UNIT OVERVIEW (Teacher Only)

Central Idea (from the text)

Hip-Hop is a cultural creation that functions as **expression, education, influence, and power**. While it began as a voice for the oppressed, its commercialization and misdirection now contribute to the continuation of miseducation when culture is exploited rather than protected.

Author's Purpose

Cedric A. Washington examines Hip-Hop as a global force rooted in Black culture, exposing how **industry control, language normalization, and glorification of destructive behavior** influence intelligence and behavior in Black communities, while calling for cultural responsibility and conscience.

STANDARDS ALIGNMENT (District-Ready)

ELA (Grades 6–8)

- Cite textual evidence to analyze informational text
- Determine central ideas and trace their development
- Analyze how examples and references shape meaning
- Write arguments supported with textual evidence
- Engage in collaborative academic discussions

Social Studies

- Examine culture as a social force
- Analyze economic exploitation and power
- Understand media influence on behavior

- Evaluate cultural continuity and change

Knowledge of SELF Alignment

SELF Mastery Focus:

- **SELF Conscience** (identity, awareness)
- **Social Conscience** (cultural responsibility)
- **Aspirations** (purpose, leadership)

TEXT SEGMENTATION (NO EDITS)

Excerpt A — Cultural Origins

- "Since 2017, Hip-Hop has been the number 1 music genre…"
- "1973 in the boogie down Bronx…"

Excerpt B — Voice of the Oppressed

- "Hip-Hop as the black CNN…"
- "Fuck Tha Police…"

Excerpt C — Industry & Exploitation

- "master and slave…"
- "…owning intellectual property…"

Excerpt D — House Negro vs. Field Negro

- "House Negro vs. Field Negro…"
- "…selling your people out…"

Excerpt E — Language & Identity

- "nigger (nigga)…"
- "…we are not negroes…"

Excerpt F — Call to Conscience

- "Hip-Hop is our culture…"
- "Wake yo' ass up!"

VOCABULARY

(Words and phrases appear directly in Chapter 6)

Students determine meaning from context in the text.

Word / Phrase	Context-Based Meaning
Hip-Hop	Cultural movement and music genre
expression	Sharing reality through art
oppression	Systemic mistreatment
global	Worldwide reach
exploitation	Unfair use for profit
master	Owner of original recordings
slave	Copies produced from the original
intellectual property	Ownership of creative work
industry	Business controlling music
House Negro	Obedient figure benefiting from system
Field Negro	Resistant and rebellious figure
privilege	Access and benefit denied to others
glorification	Praising destructive behavior
influence	Power to shape thinking
conscience	Moral awareness
culture	Shared values and practices
narrative	Story being told
identity	Understanding of who one is
cognitive dissonance	Conflicting beliefs
propaganda	Manipulated messaging
miseducation	Harmful conditioning

CLOSE READING QUESTIONS

(All responses must cite Chapter 6 directly)

Literal Understanding

1. Where and when does Washington identify the creation of Hip-Hop?
2. How does the author explain Hip-Hop's influence beyond music?

Author's Craft & Language

3. Why does Washington discuss the terms **"master"** and **"slave"** in the music industry?
4. How does the **House Negro vs. Field Negro** analogy apply to Hip-Hop artists?

Structural & Argument Analysis

5. How does Washington connect music to behavior and environment?
6. Why does the author argue that Hip-Hop must be protected as culture?

IDEAL RESPONSES (TEXT-DEPENDENT)

- Washington identifies Hip-Hop's creation in **1973 in the Bronx**.
- Hip-Hop influenced **fashion, language, politics, and global culture**.
- "Master" and "slave" reveal exploitation and ownership imbalance.
- The **House Negro** analogy describes artists who profit while harming their community.
- Music sets mood and behavior, influencing intelligence and choices.
- Hip-Hop must be protected because it is **African American culture**.

WRITING TASKS

Constructed Response

Prompt:
Explain how Cedric A. Washington describes the role of Hip-Hop in shaping intelligence and behavior. Use evidence from Chapter 6.

Extended Argument

Prompt:
Using Chapter 6, argue whether Hip-Hop today empowers or miseducates youth. Support your claim with textual evidence.

DISCUSSION PROTOCOL

Anchor Question:

"Is Hip-Hop teaching or selling culture?"

Guidelines:

- Cite the text
- Use Washington's language
- Focus on culture, not personalities

ASSESSMENT RUBRIC — Chapter 6

Category	Points
Textual Evidence	10
Understanding of Hip-Hop	10
Vocabulary in Context	5
Critical Reasoning	5
Total	**30**

TEACHER FACILITATION NOTES

- Maintain balance: acknowledge creation and critique exploitation
- Emphasize culture over entertainment
- Allow respectful disagreement grounded in text
- Reinforce responsibility with influence

KNOWLEDGE OF SELF CONNECTION

- **SELF Conscience:** Cultural identity and awareness
- **Social Conscience:** Responsibility to community
- **Aspirations:** Purpose beyond profit

Middle School TEACHER'S EDITION

Chapter 7 — Politics

The Miseducation of the Negro in the 21st Century
Teach Like Ced Series
Knowledge of SELF (Social Empowerment Learning Framework)
Grade Band: 6–8

UNIT OVERVIEW (Teacher Only)

Central Idea (from the text)

Politics in America has repeatedly promised **liberty and justice for all** while historically denying Black people sustained access to **power, opportunity, employment, and justice**. Party affiliation alone has not resolved these conditions, resulting in continued miseducation and political dependency.

Author's Purpose

Cedric A. Washington analyzes how **political parties, voting, symbolism, and representation** have failed to produce a unified Black agenda, urging collective organization, economic control, and cultural unity beyond partisan loyalty.

STANDARDS ALIGNMENT (District-Ready)

ELA (Grades 6–8)

- Cite textual evidence to analyze informational text
- Determine central ideas and trace development
- Analyze how historical references support claims
- Write arguments using evidence from the text
- Engage in structured, text-based discussion

Social Studies

- Analyze civic ideals and political systems
- Examine voting rights and representation
- Understand cause-and-effect in political history

- Evaluate power, participation, and accountability

Knowledge of SELF Alignment

SELF Mastery Focus:

- **SELF Governing** (decision-making, independence)
- **Social Conscience** (unity, collective responsibility)
- **Aspirations** (community advancement)

TEXT SEGMENTATION (NO EDITS)

Excerpt A — Civic Ideals

- "I pledge allegiance to the flag…"
- "…with liberty and justice for all."

Excerpt B — Voting & History

- Jim Crow laws (1865–1968)
- Voting Rights Act (1965)

Excerpt C — Political Parties

- Republican and Democratic leadership
- "…still asking for opportunities, employment, and justice."

Excerpt D — Representation & Symbolism

- First Black president
- First Black woman Vice President

Excerpt E — Economic Power

- "The power of the black dollar…"
- "…start the process of a Black Wall Street…"

Excerpt F — Call to Unity

- "…we must organize and construct on our own…"
- "…the time is now…"

VOCABULARY

(Words and phrases appear directly in Chapter 7)

Students determine meaning from context in the text.

Word / Phrase	Context-Based Meaning
pledge	Promise of loyalty
liberty	Freedom
justice	Fair treatment
Jim Crow	Laws enforcing segregation
civil rights	Legal freedoms
right to vote	Political participation
Democratic	Political party
Republican	Political party
representation	Being politically visible
agenda	Collective plan
unity	Togetherness
organization	Collective structure
employment	Work opportunities
opportunities	Access to advancement
justice	Fairness under the law
figurative glass ceiling	Invisible limits
socio-economic	Social and economic status
black dollar	Economic spending power
patronize	Support financially
independence	Self-sufficiency
collective	Acting together
culture	Shared identity and values

CLOSE READING QUESTIONS

(All responses must cite Chapter 7 directly)

Literal Understanding

1. According to Washington, what promise does the Pledge of Allegiance make?
2. What historical barriers prevented Black people from voting?

Author's Craft & Language

3. Why does Washington repeatedly list terms such as "Negro," "Black," and "African American"?
4. How does the phrase **"still asking for opportunities, employment, and justice"** reinforce the argument?

Structural & Argument Analysis

5. Why does Washington argue that party loyalty has not solved Black issues?
6. How does the author connect economic power to political independence?

IDEAL RESPONSES (TEXT-DEPENDENT)

- The Pledge promises **liberty and justice for all**, which Washington argues has not been fully realized.
- Jim Crow laws prevented voting and equal participation.
- The repeated naming shows different historical labels imposed on Black people.
- Despite representation, core issues remain unresolved.
- Party loyalty keeps Black people dependent rather than organized.
- Economic control allows communities to build independence and power.

WRITING TASKS

Constructed Response

Prompt:
Explain how Cedric A. Washington critiques political parties in Chapter 7. Use evidence from the text.

Extended Argument

Prompt:
Using Chapter 7, argue whether voting alone can create change. Support your argument with textual evidence.

DISCUSSION PROTOCOL

Anchor Question:

"Why does Washington believe a Black agenda must be independent of political parties?"

Guidelines:

- Cite the text directly
- Use Washington's terminology
- Focus on systems, not individuals

ASSESSMENT RUBRIC — Chapter 7

Category	Points
Textual Evidence	10
Understanding of Politics	10
Vocabulary in Context	5
Critical Reasoning	5
Total	**30**

TEACHER FACILITATION NOTES

- Emphasize civic literacy over party promotion
- Maintain neutrality while analyzing systems
- Reinforce historical continuity
- Encourage respectful, evidence-based dialogue

KNOWLEDGE OF SELF CONNECTION

- **SELF Governing:** Independent decision-making
- **Social Conscience:** Collective responsibility
- **Aspirations:** Community advancement

Middle School TEACHER'S EDITION

Chapter 8 — The Black Church

The Miseducation of the Negro in the 21st Century
Teach Like Ced Series
Knowledge of SELF (Social Empowerment Learning Framework)
Grade Band: 6–8

UNIT OVERVIEW (Teacher Only)

Central Idea (from the text)

The Black Church has historically functioned as both a source of hope and a tool of control. When faith is separated from action, historical truth, and political consciousness, it contributes to the continued miseducation of the so-called African American people.

Author's Purpose

Cedric A. Washington critiques how Christianity, religious doctrine, and church structure have been used to **pacify, divide, and spiritually condition** Black communities, while calling for truth, historical awareness, and collective responsibility.

STANDARDS ALIGNMENT (District-Ready)

ELA (Grades 6–8)

- Cite textual evidence to analyze informational text
- Determine central ideas and trace development
- Analyze how historical and religious references shape meaning
- Write arguments supported with textual evidence
- Engage in collaborative, evidence-based discussion

Social Studies

- Examine religion as a social institution
- Analyze historical power structures
- Understand cause-and-effect relationships
- Evaluate how belief systems influence behavior and politics

Knowledge of SELF Alignment

SELF Mastery Focus:

- **SELF Conscience** (truth, identity, awareness)
- **Social Conscience** (community responsibility)
- **SELF Governing** (critical thinking)

TEXT SEGMENTATION (NO EDITS)

Excerpt A — Control of the Mind

- "Keep the body and destroy the mind…"
- "…cognitive dissonance…"

Excerpt B — Religion and Oppression

- "The miseducation of the negro…"
- "…same religion as their oppressor."

Excerpt C — Christianity and Slavery

- Ephesians 6:5–6
- Slave preachers and obedience

Excerpt D — Resistance and Leadership

- Nat Turner
- Dr. Martin Luther King Jr.
- Malcolm X and Elijah Muhammad

Excerpt E — Church and Politics

- 501(c)(3) restrictions
- Separation of church and state

Excerpt F — Call to Awakening

- "The black church has forgotten…"
- "…the revelation is here."

VOCABULARY

(Words and phrases appear directly in Chapter 8)

Students determine meaning from context in the text.

Word / Phrase	Context-Based Meaning
manipulation	Control through influence
worship	Religious practice
spiritual beliefs	Faith-based convictions
cognitive dissonance	Conflicting beliefs
oppressor	One who controls others
doctrine	Religious rules
obedience	Submission to authority
uprising	Organized resistance
assassination	Killing of leaders
denomination	Branch of religion
separation of church and state	Division of religion and government
tax-exempt	Not required to pay taxes
501(c)(3)	Legal classification of churches
political campaign activity	Supporting or opposing candidates
communal effort	Working together
individualistic prosperity	Focus on personal gain
illusion	False belief
revelation	Truth becoming known
nation of people	Collective identity
miseducation	Harmful conditioning

CLOSE READING QUESTIONS

(All responses must cite Chapter 8 directly)

Literal Understanding

1. How does Washington describe the role of religion during slavery?
2. According to the text, why can't churches speak on political candidates?

Author's Craft & Language

3. Why does Washington reference Ephesians 6:5–6?
4. How does the phrase **"keep the body and destroy the mind"** frame the chapter?

Structural & Argument Analysis

5. How does Washington compare different Black leaders' religious approaches?
6. Why does the author argue the Black Church is the "biggest culprit" of miseducation?

IDEAL RESPONSES (TEXT-DEPENDENT)

- Religion was used to teach obedience and discourage resistance.
- Churches are restricted due to 501(c)(3) tax-exempt status.
- Ephesians 6:5–6 shows how scripture was used to justify slavery.
- The phrase frames psychological control.
- Leaders used faith differently, but all faced resistance and violence.
- The church separated faith from truth and action, leading to miseducation.

WRITING TASKS

Constructed Response

Prompt:
Explain how Cedric A. Washington critiques the role of the Black Church in Chapter 8. Use evidence from the text.

Extended Argument

Prompt:
Using Chapter 8, argue whether faith without action can create freedom. Support your argument with textual evidence.

DISCUSSION PROTOCOL

Anchor Question:

"Can faith liberate people if history is ignored?"

Guidelines:

- Cite the text directly
- Focus on ideas, not beliefs
- Maintain respectful academic tone

ASSESSMENT RUBRIC — Chapter 8

Category	Points
Textual Evidence	10
Understanding of Religion's Role	10
Vocabulary in Context	5
Critical Reasoning	5
Total	**30**

TEACHER FACILITATION NOTES

- Approach discussions with sensitivity and structure
- Reinforce critical thinking, not belief-shaming
- Emphasize history alongside faith
- Maintain text-centered analysis

KNOWLEDGE OF SELF CONNECTION

- **SELF Conscience:** Truth and identity
- **SELF Governing:** Independent thinking
- **Social Conscience:** Collective responsibility

Middle School TEACHER'S EDITION

Chapter 9 — Revelation (Four Hundred Years Are Up)

The Miseducation of the Negro in the 21st Century
Teach Like Ced Series
Knowledge of SELF (Social Empowerment Learning Framework)
Grade Band: 6–8

UNIT OVERVIEW (Teacher Only)

Central Idea (from the text)

Revelation is the uncovering of truth through history, scripture, lived experience, and collective awakening. After four hundred years of oppression, miseducation, and identity confusion, truth is being revealed and the miseducation of the so-called African American is being disrupted.

Author's Purpose

Cedric A. Washington synthesizes **history, scripture, politics, education, culture, and global events** to argue that the miseducation of the Negro has reached a breaking point. Through revelation, people can reclaim identity, purpose, and destiny.

STANDARDS ALIGNMENT (District-Ready)

ELA (Grades 6–8)

- Cite textual evidence to support analysis
- Determine central ideas and how they develop
- Analyze how historical and religious references support claims
- Write arguments grounded in informational text
- Engage in academic discussions using evidence

Social Studies

- Analyze historical narratives and power
- Examine cause-and-effect across time
- Understand identity, displacement, and nationhood
- Evaluate systems of control and resistance

Knowledge of SELF Alignment

SELF Mastery Focus:

- **SELF Conscience** (identity, truth, awareness)
- **SELF Governing** (independent thinking)
- **Aspirations** (purpose, destiny)

TEXT SEGMENTATION (NO EDITS)

Excerpt A — Defining Miseducation

- Merriam-Webster definition
- "poor, wrong, or harmful education"

Excerpt B — Scripture and History

- Deuteronomy 28
- Old and New Testament references

Excerpt C — Church and State

- Separation of church and state
- Use of the Bible in government

Excerpt D — Four Hundred Years

- 1619 Jamestown
- COVID-19 pandemic
- George Floyd

Excerpt E — Identity and Awakening

- Cognitive dissonance
- Naming and origin
- Revelation

Excerpt F — Call to Destiny

- Chosen people
- Reparations
- Cultural responsibility
- Knowledge of SELF

VOCABULARY

(Words and phrases appear directly in Chapter 9)

Students determine meaning from context in the text.

Word / Phrase	Context-Based Meaning
revelation	Truth becoming known
miseducation	Poor, wrong, or harmful education
cognitive dissonance	Conflicting beliefs
separation of church and state	Division of religion and government
doctrine	Religious teaching
interpretation	Personal understanding
scripture	Biblical text
Old Testament	Early biblical writings
New Testament	Later biblical writings
Deuteronomy	Biblical book
curse	Consequence described in scripture
four hundred years	Length of oppression
pandemic	Global sickness
uprising	Collective resistance
awakening	Conscious realization
identity	Understanding of origin
chosen people	Designated nation
reparations	Compensation owed
destiny	Purpose and future
culture	Shared identity
intelligence	Ability to apply knowledge
behavior	Actions shaped by intelligence

CLOSE READING QUESTIONS

(All responses must cite Chapter 9 directly)

Literal Understanding

1. How does Washington define miseducation?

2. What does the author identify as the starting point of African American history in mainstream education?

Author's Craft & Language

3. Why does Washington connect COVID-19 and George Floyd to revelation?
4. How does the phrase **"four hundred years are up"** shape the chapter's message?

Structural & Argument Analysis

5. How does scripture function as historical evidence in this chapter?
6. Why does Washington argue revelation is happening now?

IDEAL RESPONSES (TEXT-DEPENDENT)

- Miseducation is defined as poor, wrong, or harmful education.
- History is taught as beginning with slavery.
- COVID-19 and George Floyd exposed global injustice.
- "Four hundred years are up" signals an end to tolerance and ignorance.
- Scripture explains displacement, curses, and identity.
- Revelation occurs as people reconnect to history and truth.

WRITING TASKS

Constructed Response

Prompt:
Explain how Cedric A. Washington defines revelation in Chapter 9. Use evidence from the text.

Extended Argument

Prompt:
Using Chapter 9, argue why Washington believes the miseducation of the Negro is being disrupted now. Support your response with textual evidence.

DISCUSSION PROTOCOL

Anchor Question:

"What happens when people learn the truth about who they are?"

Guidelines:

- Cite the text directly
- Focus on ideas, not personal beliefs
- Maintain academic respect

ASSESSMENT RUBRIC — Chapter 9

Category	Points
Textual Evidence	10
Understanding of Revelation	10
Vocabulary in Context	5
Critical Reasoning	5
Total	**30**

TEACHER FACILITATION NOTES

- Emphasize synthesis of earlier chapters
- Reinforce evidence-based discussion
- Avoid speculation beyond the text
- Frame revelation as learning, not debate

KNOWLEDGE OF SELF CONNECTION

- **SELF Conscience:** Truth and identity
- **SELF Governing:** Independent thought
- **Aspirations:** Purpose and destiny

APPENDIX A — Academic Standards Alignment (ELA & Social Studies)

English Language Arts (Grades 6–8)

Aligned to **informational text, argumentation, and discussion**.

Students will:

- Cite **textual evidence** to support analysis of informational texts
- Determine **central ideas** and track their development across chapters
- Analyze how an author uses **history, scripture, and definition** to support claims
- Write **arguments and explanatory texts** grounded in evidence
- Engage in **collaborative discussions** using accountable talk

Text-Based Skills Emphasized:

- Definition analysis (miseducation, revelation, knowledge, intelligence)
- Cause and effect (culture → intelligence → behavior)
- Author's purpose and perspective
- Historical and religious references as informational sources

Social Studies Alignment

Students will:

- Examine **historical narratives and power structures**
- Analyze **systems of oppression and resistance**
- Understand **identity, displacement, and nationhood**
- Evaluate **continuity and change over time**
- Interpret **primary and secondary sources** embedded in text

Key Social Studies Themes from the Text:

- Slavery and post-slavery America
- Jim Crow and Civil Rights
- Education systems
- Political participation
- Religion and governance
- Community and culture

APPENDIX B — Knowledge of S.E.L.F. Alignment Map

All chapters intentionally align to the **five SELF Mastery areas** already named in your curriculum.

SELF Domain	Textual Evidence
SELF Conscience	Identity, revelation, miseducation, culture
SELF Governing	Independent thinking, rejecting imposed narratives
Social Conscience	Community responsibility, collective action
Aspirations	Destiny, purpose, future generations
Good People Skills	Leadership, accountability, unity

APPENDIX C — Vocabulary Protocol (Text-Faithful)

Instructional Rule:
All vocabulary **must come directly from the text**. Students derive meaning through **context, discussion, and reference**, not memorization.

Vocabulary Instruction Method:

1. Identify word in text
2. Locate sentence and paragraph
3. Discuss meaning using author's words
4. Confirm with dictionary **only if cited in text** (Oxford, Merriam-Webster)

Examples from the Text:

- miseducation
- revelation
- cognitive dissonance
- culture
- intelligence
- behavior
- doctrine
- interpretation
- separation of church and state
- oppression
- liberation
- destiny

APPENDIX D — Assessment Philosophy

Assessment is NOT:

- Rote memorization
- Opinion-based journaling without evidence
- Compliance-driven worksheets

Assessment IS:

- Text-based reasoning
- Evidence-driven writing
- Academic discussion
- Critical reflection grounded in reading

APPENDIX E — Universal Writing Rubric (Grades 6–8)

Category	Points
Use of Textual Evidence	10
Accuracy of Interpretation	10
Vocabulary Usage (from text)	5
Organization & Clarity	5
Total	**30 Points**

APPENDIX F — Discussion Norms (District-Safe)

- Speak from the **text**, not personal attack
- Respect differing interpretations
- Cite page/section when possible
- Listen actively
- Participation is encouraged, not forced

APPENDIX G — Teacher Positioning Statement

This Teacher's Edition:

- Centers **academic literacy**
- Meets **ELA and Social Studies standards**
- Supports **SEL development**
- Uses **informational text analysis**
- Encourages **critical thinking without indoctrination**

Instruction is **standards-aligned**, **culturally responsive**, and **academically rigorous**.

APPENDIX H — Implementation Readiness Checklist

District-appropriate language
Standards alignment documented
SEL integration embedded
No supplemental ideology required
Text-dependent instruction only
Suitable for Grades 6–8

www.ingramcontent.com/pod-product-compliance
Lightning Source LLC
Chambersburg PA
CBHW061757260326
41914CB00006B/1138